RADHA SOAMI MAT PRAKASH

OR

A BRIEF VIEW OF RADHA SOAMI FAITH,

BEING

A MESSAGE OF ETERNAL PEACE AND JOY TO ALL NATIONS.

RADHA SOAMI MAT PRAKASH

OR

A BRIEF VIEW OF RADHA SOAMI FAITH,

BEING

A MESSAGE OF ETERNAL PEACE AND JOY TO ALL NATIONS.

BY

HUZUR MAHARAJ

GYAN

Published by

Gyan Publishing House
5, Ansari Road
Daryaganj, New Delhi-110002
Phone: 011-47034999, 9811692060
E-mail: books@gyanbooks.com

Distribution Network
gyanbooks.com
India, USA, Canada, UK, Australia

ISBN: 978-93-6433-017-6 (HB)
First Published, 1896

2nd Impression 2024

Printed at: Gyan Press, Delhi.

RADHA SOAMI MAT PRAKASH OR A BRIEF VIEW OF RADHA SOAMI FAITH..
AUTHOR: HUZUR MAHARAJ

RÁDHÁ SOÁMI MAT PRAKÁSH.

RÁDHÁ SOÁMI MAT PRAKÁSH

OR

A BRIEF VIEW OF RÁDHÁ SOÁMI FAITH,

BEING

A MESSAGE OF ETERNAL PEACE AND JOY TO ALL NATIONS.

PUBLISHED UNDER THE AUTHORITY

OF

RAI SALIG RAM BAHADUR OF AGRA,
Retired Postmaster-General, N. W. P.

BENARES:
THE CHANDRAPRABHA PRESS CO. LD.

1896.

First Edition 1500 Copies. *Price 10 Ans.*

CONTENTS.

RÁDHÁ SOÁMI SAHÁI.

PREFACE.

1. This tract is intended for the benefit of those who, seeing the instability and transitory state of the things in this world, as well as its short-lived pleasures and greatness, have a craving for everlasting and unalloyed happiness and undisturbed peace in a mansion which is not subject to change, decay or dissolution.

2. It will also help sincere enquirers of truth who, observing that the love or affection for objects in this world is attended with great pain and affliction consequent on their separation or disappearance, are anxious to know the Supreme and Eternal Cause, or Creator and Master of the whole creation, with a view to fix their attention and set their heart entirely on His Holy Feet, and approach Him in His Highest Mansion.

3. This class of thinkers and enquirers conclude from their observation of the numerous gradations in the creation, and the laws which govern the movements of heavenly bodies, that there must be a

highest sphere all pure, a boundless ocean of love and spirit, the residence of the Supreme Being, the Eternal and Unchangeable, the Supreme Master and Director of the whole creation, that every human being (who is a drop from that Ocean) should aspire to, and try proper means to approach.

4. These means have been prescribed by the Supreme Being Himself when He appeared in human form with the merciful object of reclaiming down-trodden humanity involved in endless troubles and misery in this world. They can be easily practised by both men and women of any age and in all countries, who, observing the perishable nature of all objects in these regions, have the slightest but sincere desire of finding truth and enjoying eternal joy and bliss in the highest and purest regions of love and spirit in the August and Happy Presence of their Supreme Father.

RÁHDÁ SOÁMI DAYÁL KÍ DAYÁ

RÁDHÁ SOÁMI SAHÁI.

(*GRANT MERCIFUL RÁDHÁ SOÁMI THY GRACE & PROTECTION.*)

A BRIEF VIEW OF RÁDHÁ SOÁMI FAITH.

Rádhá Soámi the holy name of the Supreme Being.

1. The Rádhá Soámi *mat* or faith derives its name from its original Founder, the Supreme Being, Rádhá Soámi who appeared in this world in human form and designated Himself *Sant Satgurú* or perfect Saint or true Guide and Preceptor, and preached holy doctrines to sincere enquirers of Truth for the deliverance of their spirit from the bondage of body and its surroundings, as well as from the pains and pleasures of this world, and for the ultimate admission (of their spirit) into the Holy Presence of the Supreme Being after traversing

and breaking through the trammels and impediments in the material spheres.

2. The Holy name Rádhá Soámi has been given out by the Supreme Being Himself. It resounds in splendid refulgence in the higher spheres and can be heard within themselves by those who perform devotion by practising *Surat Shabd Yoga* according to the instructions given by the Supreme Being Himself.

3. All obstacles thrown in the way and traps laid by Universal Mind and Matter to stop or interfere with the progress of a pilgrim to the high mansion of the Supreme Being in pure spiritual regions disappear at once on the pronunciation of the Holy name Rádhá Soámi by the devotee: such is the immediate effect and beneficial influence exercised by this Almighty Name. It at once strikes awe and terror in the heart of the conflicting agents and revolting forces met with by the devotee while traversing the material regions and gradually removes them altogether from his path.

4. This Holy name Rádhá Soámi signifies

both the Supreme Being and the original Spirit or Sound current (or Word) which emanated from His Holy Feet, and which is the prime factor and principal agent in the whole creation.

Three Factors in Creation.

5. According to Rádhá Soámi faith there are three factors in the creation, of which the first and principal and the prime mover and life-giver is the Spirit, or Word or Sound, the second or the main working factor is Mind and the third the Matter, of which the body and senses (the instruments of action) are made. The first principle or factor, namely Spirit, is the prime cause of everything and presides over all, and has its abode in the uppermost regions above all and beyond the Mind (the second factor) in the innermost part of the body. The locality of the Mind or the second factor, is below that of spirit or outside the innermost quarter, while the flesh or body formed of Matter, the third factor, occupies the outermost portion of the vehicle or human form with the

senses attached thereto. Accordingly there are three degrees, and hence three Grand Divisions in the Universe or Macrocosm with corresponding divisions in the human body or Microcosm.

6. The three degrees or grand divisions, comprised in the entire creation, according to Rádhá Soámi faith are :–

1. Spiritual
2. Spiritual-Material
3. Material-Spiritual

Pure spirit, uncontaminated with matter, exists in the first grand division. Here the Supreme Being reigns over absolutely spiritual life. This, the purest possible form of life, has no desire but to love and serve the Supreme Being. The joys—the very existence—of this pure spirit-life are derived from the Supreme Being who is the Ocean of spirit, love and joy. Nothing concerning this degree is known or has been known to the founder of any religious creed. It comprises six sub-divisions and is called the *Dayál Desh* or the Regions of Mercy.

7. The second or Spiritual-Material degree or grand division is entirely free from all worldly passions and desires of the lower order. Likening the Supreme Being to an Ocean, the president of the second degree is a tide from that Ocean. He is a kind of Viceroy who rules over all life existing in the space comprised in the second and third grand divisions committed to his care. As its name indicates, the spiritual-material degree contains both spirit and matter. But matter is, comparatively speaking, pure and is subject to, and controlled by spirit. Life here is very pure and though clothed in pure material forms, spirit predominates. This degree also comprises six sub-divisions and is called the *Brahmand* or the regions of Universal Mind and pure matter.

8. In the third or Material-Spiritual degree matter predominates over spirit. Life is composed of spirits wholly clothed in coarse matter. Having quite forgotten the higher abode from which they originally sprang, the spirits here have acquired carnal desires and passions. This also comprises six sub-divisions and is

called the *Pind* or the regions of Individual Mind and coarse matter.

9. This degree is dominated over by a wave emanating from the Supreme Being and flowing through the tide which has already been likened to a Viceroy. This wave or current may, for want of a better name, be called a Governor who presides over the Material Universe and controls matter.

Our solar system belongs to the third degree.

10. All solar systems, like ours, are included in the third degree. Beyond all solar systems in this plane, is the locality of the second degree; beyond that locality again is the situation of the first degree, the residence of the Supreme Being.

Correspondence of Macrocosm with Microcosm.

11. The above three grand divisions in the Universe have a correspondence, or are in the same plane, with similar divisions in the human form or body which is a miniature or Microcosm of the Great Universe or Macrocosm.

The Supreme Being distinguished from the Gods of other religions.

12. The Supreme Being, as already said, is unknown. The Spirit or the Viceroy who presides over the second degree, is the Lord God of the Bible: he is the *Sat* or *Satchitánand* or *Shudh Brahm* of the *Vedántees*, the *Nirván* of the *Jains* and the *Buddhists* and the *Láhút* of the Mahomedan Saints. The Spirit or Governor who rules over the third degree is the *Brahm* or *Parmátmá* or God of most religions in the world.

The second and third degrees contain spirit and matter; the former predominates in the second, and the latter in the third degree.

13. The entire creation below the first degree is composed of two parts, namely, spirit which is all good and pure, and matter which is always more or less bad. Man is a drop from the Ocean, that is, the Supreme Being. This drop of pure good spirit is so mixed with matter that it becomes in bondage thereto, and unless aided by a Superior Spirit is always

liable
to yield to temptation and deteriorate or sink down in matter.

16. There are two streams in our solar system ; the one ever improving, the other always deteriorating. The spirits of the first of these streams pass from plants through the lower creation till they reach man; they then become angels or heavenly spirits and ultimately merge into the Supreme Being or remain in His Presence. Maintenance of indi\dduality in the changes later than man depends upon the practice of devotion according to Surat Sabd Yoga or the union of the Spirit with the Word — the Word being the emanation from the Supreme Being. If such devotion be not practised, the spirit loses its previous individuality and becomes merged into a lower stage fit for its reception. A devotee, w^hen merged into the Supreme Being, can assume his individuality at liable
to yield to temptation and deteriorate or sink down in matter.

16. There are two streams in our solar system ; the one ever improving, the other always deteriorating. The spirits of the first of these streams pass from plants through the lower creation till they reach man; they then become angels or heavenly spirits and ultimately merge into the Supreme Being or remain in His Presence. Maintenance of indi\dduality in the changes later than man depends upon the practice of devotion according to Surat Sabd Yoga or the union of the Spirit with the Word – the Word being the emanation from the Supreme Being. If such devotion be not practised, the spirit loses its previous individuality and becomes merged into a lower stage fit for its reception. A devotee, w^hen merged into the Supreme Being, can assume his individuality at

pleasure. Such a being is called a perfect *Sant*, a Special and Beloved Son of the Supreme Being. But the spirits who belong to the deteriorating stream are wholly under the influence of matter. At every change they get lower and lower until they reach the lowest form in the creation.

The Special and Beloved Sons of the Supreme Being or Sants.

17. The Supreme Being has Special and Beloved Sons called *Sants* and *Param Sants*, who are full of mercy and love and who descend periodically upon the earth to deliver spirits from the bondage of matter and to carry them to the Presence of the Supreme Father.

One should look for a Sant or Sádh to approach the Supreme Being.

18. Any one desirous of reaching the Supreme Being must search for a *Sant Satgurú* (incarnation of the Supreme Being) or a *Sádh Gurú* (one who has reached the top of the second grand division) and invoke His help, and receive instructions from one of these Superior Guides, as to the manner of his devotion and procedure.

Definition of Sant Satgurú.

19. A *Sant Satgurú* is He who has either descended directly from the Highest Division or reached that quarter by practice of *Surat Shabd Yoga* under the immediate direction of the former.

Definition of Sádh Gurú and Satsangí.

20. A *Sádh Gurú* is He who has descended from the top of the second grand division or reached it by the practice of *Surat Shabd Yoga* under the direction of a *Sant Satgurú* and is proceeding towards the highest division. A *Satsangí* is he who having full belief and confidence in the *Sant Satgurú* and His words, is practising *Surat Shabd Yoga* under His immediate direction and having traversed some distance is pushing on upwards.

The Supreme Being is both personal and impersonal.

21. The name of the Supreme Being is *Rádhá Soámi*. He is impersonal, but personal in the second and third divisions and when He manifests Himself through humanity as *Sant Satgurú*. His attributes are mostly met with

in the *Sant Satgurú*, who might be called an incarnation of *Sat Purush Rádhá Soámi*, the *true* Supreme Being.

Definition of true salvation.

22. The deliverance of spirit from the bondage of body, senses and mind, and its gradual ascension and eventual entrance into the first or highest division by the practice of *Surat Shabd Yoga* is perfect salvation according to Rádhá Soámi faith.

At present the *Surat* or spirit which is a particle of the Supreme Being or a ray from the Supreme Sun or a drop from the Supreme Ocean of spirit, having descended from the highest or first region has become encased in material coverings, and in a manner intermingled with matter and is in this, the third region, subject to the forces or carnal desires and passions resulting from such mixture.

Spirit subject to birth and re-birth in the second and third degrees.

23. In its descent from the highest region the spirit has become enveloped in various coverings of matter or bodies, and as long as it

remains in the second and third divisions where matter exists, it cannot be freed from re-birth in the lower or higher regions. It is only in the first or highest division where there is no matter, that there is no re-birth.

Rádhá Soámí faith not built on the scriptures of any religion—The efficacy of Surat Shabd Yoga testified by inspired religions.

24. Rádha Soámi faith is not built on the basis of scriptures appertaining to Hindu or any other religion, but on the precepts or instructions of the Supreme Being Himself, Who appeared on this earth in human form and graciously performed the functions of a *Sant Satgurú* for the benefit of degraded humanity. The original books of all inspired religions, however, bear sufficient testimony to the superiority and efficacy of the *Surat Shabd Yoga* as the only means and the only highway to the Highest Heaven.

The internal sound current is the means of raising the spirit. Difference of Dhunyátmak and Varnátmak names. The power of sound current or Shabd.

25. The sound heard internally is a current

which has originally emanated from the Supreme Being and is the means not only of concentrating the will but also of raising the spirit to the source from which it emanated.

26. At the time of initiation, a novice receives instructions as regards the particulars of the *Shabd* of each sub-division by means of which he has to raise his spirit upwards. This is called *Dhunyátmak* name, while that uttered by tongue is called *Varnátmak* name.

27. It must be clearly understood that by *Shabd* or Word or internal voice is meant the spirit or life current which enlivens every part of the body and is the main principle or essence which supports life in and gives activity to every being or body in the whole creation or Universe. Even in this world every thing is done by means of word or sound, and all affairs are managed through its instrumentality, as one speaks or gives order and the other attends to it or carries it out into execution. The instantaneous effect of word or sound on human beings and even animals is so apparent

in every day experience of our life that it needs no further explanation.

The state of spirit in the third degree—The change of its powers with the change of its spheres.

28. At present the spirit of man is residing in the third or material-spiritual region, and has, therefore, to do all the work here by means of the senses and the mind which are mediums between it and the material objects, and consequently, as a natural result, its power has become quite hampered. But as soon as it begins to ascend, the powers which are now lying dormant, become active and the spirit acquires ultra-material or higher powers.

The method for taking back the spirit to its original source is to ride the sound current.

29. The method for taking back the spirit to its Supreme source is first to concentrate at the focus of the eyes, the spirit and mind which are diffused in our body and in a manner tied to external objects by desires and passions, and next to commence its journey homewards by attending to the internal

sound, or in other words, by riding the life or sound current which has originally emanated from the Supreme source.

30. The current which has been instrumental in having brought it down here must naturally be the only true path for its return to the original source, and whoever finds this current is on the path of emancipation. This current which is the spirit and life current, is called in the Rádhá Soámi faith, Sound or Word or Holy Name.

Testimony of sound as given by other religions.

31. Other extant religions give also distant allusion to this life or sound current; for instance in the Bible we find, "In the beginning was the Word, and the Word was with God, and the Word was God." The *Vedás* have also *Nád* or Word, the *Praṇava* (प्रणव) or *Om* (ओम्) and so others.

The Shabd of Rádhá Soámi faith distinguished from that of other religions.

32. But there is a difference between the Word or Sound which is alluded to in the different extant religions and that in Rádhá Soámi

faith. Their information is not confined to the Word or Sound of one and the same sphere. Some belong to the spiritual-material and some to material-spiritual regions. While the Word or Sound mentioned by Rádhá Soámi faith appertains to the first or highest spiritual sphere. These sounds are not nominal words or names like the names of common things, but are real sounds resounding in their appropriate spheres like the ringing sound of bell, shell, &c.

The efficacy of the real name or sound to approach the centre from which it emanates.

33. By merely repeating a name or word, the thing or substance which it designates or to which it appertains cannot be acquired, but by hearing a real Word or Sound, the centre from which that sound is emanating can be approached. You cannot obtain bread by simply repeating the word "bread" unless you go to a baker's shop and purchase it there.

34. So by internal repetition of *real holy words or names* one can only collect together at the focus of the eyes, the spirit which is

diffused all over the body, but by internally hearing the sounds thereof, one can actually hold communion with, and gradually approach the centres whence these Holy Sounds or names emanate.

Necessity of sincere prayer.

35. Prayer is necessary to obtain blessing and mercy to help man's perfect salvation, but it must be offered from the inmost of heart and not confined to mere utterance. It must also be backed up by works of faith and charity performed through love and affection for the Supreme Being.

Necessity of sincere love for the Supreme Being.

36. Great stress is laid in the Rádhá Soámi faith on engendering love for the Supreme Being. This can only be done when all worldly desires are gradually eradicated from the mind, and it becomes impressed to the inmost core, with the unbounded bliss that might be attained by approaching the Supreme Being, Rádhá Soámi. Love being attraction, it is quite plain that the devotional practice for approaching the

Supreme Being will become very easy indeed, if there is true love for Him, and devotion, instead of being a thing of duty, will be the highest and most blissful work in this world.

Necessary restrictions as regards mode of living.

37. In following this mode of devotion the following restrictions are made with regard to diet and mode of living. No intoxicating drink or drug and animal food is to be taken and immoderate indulgence in any desire is to be avoided. Animal food is forbidden on account of its producing a material tendency in human nature, and intoxicating drink is detrimental to a calm and natural state of the brain and the nervous system. Other public and private duties should be carried on as usual.

Definition of good and bad acts.

38. The moral code appertaining to Rádhá Soámi faith is comprised in two sentences :–

(1) All acts including spiritual practice which tend to free the spirit from matter and raise it towards its source are good works.

(2) All acts which tend to degrade the spirit by weighing it downwards deeper and deeper into matter are bad works. Again any action done with a view to help the needy from unselfish motives is good work; and the contrary, bad work in this world.

39. Rádhá Soámi Dayál says that the highest aim and object of every spirit should be to gradually throw off the coatings of matter with a view to return to the Supreme Source. This is what He defines as "good." To seek worldly objects, to set the heart entirely on worldly affairs is a retrograde movement; and this is "bad." The next aim of every human being should be to do good to his fellow creatures by thought, word and deed as far as practicable, and to avoid injuring them except in the interests of society or for the good of many.

Brotherhood of Rádhá Soámi faith—place of worship—offering of flower garland.

40. Priests in the ordinary acceptation

of the term find no place in Rádhá Soámi religion. All the followers are originally equal and form one big brotherhood or fraternity. But the superiority of each member depends on the degree of love which he imbibes for the Supreme Being, and on the intensity of the desire he manifests to approach Him. The more fervent members receive inspiration and preach to others giving them also counsel. There are no temples and no shrines. Any house or even open air is equally fit for the purpose of worship. No place is more holy than another except where the *Sant Satgurú* resided while on earth. Each member of a congregation assembled for worship brings a wreath of flowers which he places round the neck of the Preacher. Immediately or at the close of the service or *Sat Sang*, this wreath is returned to him and sanctity thus obtained.

Rádhá Soámi faith consists in four words.

41. The Rádhá Soámi faith is comprised in four words viz.:—

(1) *Sant Satgurú.*

(2) *Sat Shabd* or *Sat Nám.*

(3) *Satsang*

(4) *Sat Anurág* or sincere love for the Supreme Being and *Sant Satgurú.*

42. (1) *Sant Satgurú.* He has already been described above.

(2) *Sat Shabd* or Holy and true name is the sound proceeding from the Original Source. It undergoes some changes, or in other words, is enveloped in a sort of covering at every step in its descent in material regions. By step is meant each sub-division or sphere.

(3) *Satsang* is attendance on the *Satgurú*, hearing His discourse, reading His works, and performing acts of faith and charity inspired by love for, and a desire to approach, the Supreme Being. This is external *Satsang.* Internal *Satsang* is the application of mind and spirit to the sound current at the time of practice and an effort to raise them to higher spheres.

(4) By sincere love is meant a strong fervent desire and perseverance to approach the Supreme Being. This desire should outweigh all worldly desires.

Superiority of Sound practice over external religious observances.

43. It is evident from thc above that all external works of charity, worship, pilgrimage, or mere reading of holy books, unless accompanied by internal practice of *Surat Shabd Yoga* (or the union of spirit and Holy Word) do not lead to true salvation which can only be attained by raising the spirit to the First Degree or pure Spiritual Regions. One may reap the fruit of such acts by obtaining happiness in the same or a new body on re-birth, in the same or a higher sphere. But to approach the Supreme Being, there is absolutely no other means except the practice of *Surat Shabd Yoga* under the guidance of a *Sant Satgurú* or a *Sadh Gurú*, or a sincere lover of the Supreme Being who has received instructions from, and is helped in his practice by one of those Superior and Holy Spirits.

Description of three natural states—wakefulness, dream, and sound sleep.

44. It is necessary to remark here that every human being passes through three states of life in every twenty four hours, viz.,

(1) The wakeful state in which he works with his senses and limbs, feels pleasure and pain, and comes in contact with other creatures and objects in this world. In this state the principal seat of the spirit is in the pupil of the eye.

(2) The dreamy state in which his connection with the corporeal body (or outer covering) and the senses as well as the external world ceases or is slackened. He has no sensation of bodily pleasure and pain, and all anxiety about worldly affairs in a manner disappears. In this state the spirit is drawn within and upwards to the astral sphere where it dreams and comes in contact with astral creation, and works by means of internal mind and senses.

(3) The state of deep and sound sleep when all action of mind and senses ceases and the spirit is drawn further inwards and its connection with both the corporeal and astral bodies temporarily ceases. Breathing and motion of the heart and pulse continue, but in

certain diseases such as catalepsy as well as in the state of deep trance &c., the motion of the heart and lungs also ceases owing to the spirit being withdrawn innermost.

45. It would thus appear that the connection of the spirit with the corporeal body and senses as well as the objects of this world is established during the wakeful state only, when the spirit current returns to its seat in the pupil of the eye where the sensation of worldly pleasure and pain is experienced, and the mind, the senses and the limbs perform their respective functions. This connection is temporarily severed when the spirit withdraws itself from its seat and all sensations and functions cease simultaneously. A similar change begins to appear when a man is dying, that is to say, his spirit current is gradually withdrawn from the extremities and when the pupil of the eye is turned upwards and inwards, the spirit flies and its connection with the body ceases for ever.

The mode of devotion as prescribed by Rádhá Soámi faith is the only means to approach the Supreme Being.

46. Rádhá Soámi faith prescribes the

means or certain mode of devotion whereby a man could at pleasure withdraw his spirit from its seat in wakeful state, and thus release it to a certain extent from the bondage of body and senses and slacken its connection with the outer world, and thus free himself to the same extent from pain and pleasure of this world, and retire temporarily to take rest and enjoy the bliss of higher spheres within himself. A man can traverse the regions of death and return to body at pleasure, or in other words, by practising devotion for a certain length of time one can withdraw his spirit to the point where death takes place and even beyond it, and can, at pleasure, bring it back to the seat occupied in the wakeful state and resume the functions of mind, body and senses.

47. The benefits accruing from such a practice viz., the enjoyment of bliss in higher regions within us and obtaining relief from the pleasures, pains and cares of this world as well as of the body &c., are self-evident proof of the great importance and extraordinary usefulness

of the mode of devotion prescribed by Rádhá Soámi faith. This mode of devotion is the only and surest means of eventually attaining perfect salvation or complete liberation from the bondage of material coatings appertaining to the lower and higher regions of matter.

48. It is rightly inferred from the above that there is no other way to raise the spirit to the highest sphere but the one prescribed by the Rádhá Soámi faith viz., removing or raising the spirit gradually from its seat in the pupil of the eye, in the same manner as it rises or withdraws at the time of death, and by catching or riding the Sound or life current to carry it back towards the main source from which it originally descended.

This mode of devotion is free from all risk and danger and can easily be practised by men and women of any age, literate or illiterate.

49. The mode of devotion referred to above is free from all dangers and is so easy of practice that a child of ten or twelve years as well as an adult and the old can perform it conveniently and comfortably at all times, without interfering

with the daily business of life. The mind of the devotee will gradually (as he progresses in his practice) imbibe more and more love for the Supreme Being, intensifying his desire to approach Him in the highest region, and look upon the pleasures and objects of this world as trifling and transitory.

Prán Yoga discarded as dangerous and unnecessary.

50. In times gone by and even now some persons consider *Prán Yoga* or the practice of suspending breath and drawing it up to the sixth or seventh nervous centre or ganglion (the seat of which is in the interior, behind the point between the two eyes) as a means for obtaining salvation. There is no doubt that this practice secures the liberation of spirit from the bondage of coarse matter in the third grand division. But in the first instance the process is very difficult and is attended with danger in case of slight omission or commission as regards its rules and conditions, and secondly, the practitioner would still remain in the regions of matter, though pure, and therefore, subject to

rebirth and the pains and troubles attendant thereon. A man living with his family and pursuing his profession can hardly comply with the rigid and strict rules laid down for this practice and even those who have renounced the world, are scarcely able to carry out this practice without permanently endangering their health, and thereby retarding their progress in the way of attaining their objects namely, the raising of spirit to the sixth or seventh *Chakra* or nervous centre.

51. Moreover the *Prán* or breath current is dependent on the Spirit or Word current for its life and support, as when the latter is drawn inward to more than ordinary extent the breathing is gradually stopped, or in other words, the *Prán* current also follows the spirit current or is withdrawn from the body, and its action gradually ceases.

52. Again the *Prán* current is a subordinate agent to the spirit current and its function is limited to certain automatic action in the body, as when the spirit current is withdrawn

during the time of sound sleep the function of senses and limbs ceases, and though the *Prán* current or breathing continues its action, it cannot exercise any influence over the senses and limbs which respond to the impulse from the spirit current only. The practice of *Prán Yoga* is, therefore, discarded by Rádhá Soámi faith as difficult, dangerous, not carrying to the highest sphere and therefore useless and unnecessary.

Evidence of the existence of God the Almighty—The essence of God and Spirit is the same—It is an emanation from Him.

53. A sincere seeker after truth should allow no doubt to remain in his mind about the existence of the Almighty Creator, as the whole creation, terrestrial and celestial, from its design and object, and the immutable laws by which it is governed, bears evidence to the existence of the all-powerful and controlling hand of an intelligent Supreme Being. His power commonly called energy is diffused everywhere, but it requires impulse from the Supreme Source to put it into action, and this

impulse is the Prime Spirit or Sound current which forming centres at certain distances completed the work of creation in each circle or system so designed, and descending in its course carried out the work of creation to the furthest limit. The lowest system is dependent upon the one higher than itself for its life and support, and this again upon one higher still and so on, until the highest sphere is reached which is the abode of the Supreme Power, the Prime Cause of the first impulse, or life and spirit current. These systems are called solar systems, each working in subordination to the higher one, and all depending for their life and support on the Supreme Being.

54. This Supreme Being is the sole master of the whole creation, and the spirits clothed in body in this Universe are emanations from Him, that is, their essence is the same, and they more or less exercise the same powers as the Supreme Being within their respective spheres or bodies viz., controlling matter or the forces of nature and elements which work harmoneously in subordination to the spirit.

The above statement illustrated.

55. To understand the above more clearly one should carefully observe and watch the progress of a plant from the time it germinates till it is fully grown up, and till it dies. Since the first manifestation of germ or spirit the forces of nature viz., attraction, repulsion, construction, chemical affinity, light, electricity and elements, including gases &c., all combine and work harmoneously to aid its growth and sustenance. Again when the spirit separates itself from the plant, the very same forces help its decay and decomposition till the body or form disappears. The same case is observable in the growth of all bodies in the Animal and Vegetable kingdoms from the time of germination or first manifestation of spirit till its separation from those bodies which results in the death, decomposition or decay of the latter.

56. It may, therefore, be inferred from the above that the spirits are emanations from the Supreme Being or the first and original cause of creation. Also that the spirits by the powers

they exercise are the means of support and sustenance of the bodies thus created, and that their separation from those bodies is the cause of their death and decay.

57. It is evident from the above that the whole work of creation in various spheres is carried on through the instrumentality of emanations or spirits issuing forth from the Supreme Being as rays from the Sun, and that this creation exists and subsists as long as the spirit maintains connection with the body or the form it assumes, and that decay and decomposition follow the severance of this connection; that matter and all forces resulting from its contact with spirit in various spheres are wholly controlled by spirit and that nothing can move or act by itself without an impulse from the spirit force which is immortal. Matter within its sphere is also imperishable in its original form namely chaotic or atomic, but it owes its life and activity to the impulse from the spirit force.

Báchak Gyán (Sophistry) and Idolatry.

58. There are people who have gone to the

one or the other extreme in forming their opinion and conducting the worship of the Deity, that is to say, some have adopted the worship of form or some sign said to have appertained to the Creator when He incarnated Himself in human form, or to one of the superior spirits who appeared in this world as prophets or mediators; while others regard Him as formless and Omnipresent and contemplate Him as *Ákásh* or ether pervading the entire creation and space.

59. According to Rádhá Soámi faith both the above schools of thinkers appear to be in fault, in as much as they exhibit utter ignorance of the real state of things, and therefore the means adopted by them for their salvation are faulty and defective. There is no doubt that the Supreme Being is formless and boundless; but when a current from this Prime Source descended into the lower sphere and in a manner animated and awakened matter, the first form produced by the admixture of the two was the image for the first time assumed by the

original spirit current, and the outlines of this form served as a standard for all the animated forms subsequently created in the various spheres below; and these outlines are also more or less distinctly visible in the forms of all creatures on this earth.

60. The saying that God created man after His own image is confirmed by the fact of his superiority over all creatures in this world, and the circumstance of the outlines of the human form being adopted with more or less precision in the structure of the whole animal kingdom. If such is the case with the human image in creation in the lower order, it follows that this very image can be traced backwards and upwards in a more and more perfect order till we reach the first form, the most perfect, originally assumed by the spirit current, when commencing the work of creation.

61. It is hopeless, therefore, for any one to approach the formless without first coming in contact with the various main forms assumed by the spirit in its descent to the lower spheres.

These are living forms ever present in the spheres to which they pertain within every human being, and they help a traveller in his onward journey to the highest and original form which again leads him to the formless, and thus perfect salvation is possible to be attained. To degrade the living form to one made of stone or metal or to stick to certain signs and symbols appertaining thereto and preparing their metallic imitation &c., &c., without the knowledge of the original or any attempt to trace it within ourselves is wandering away from real to unreal object.

62. Again to think of the formless and liken it to ether without the knowledge of the various forms or coatings which its main current or creative agency has assumed in its descent to this sphere is as faulty and irreconcilable with our present limited thoughts and ideas as the degradation of the living form to imitations made of stone or metal, like toys.

63. Some have gone to a futher extreme

and identifying themselves with the First and Eternal Cause, the formless and boundless Source of spirit, have lost all regard and consideration for the same, and become extremely selfish and proud of their existence which is a mere drop from the Ocean of Spirit and Love or a mere ray from the Supreme Sun, the Life and Light Giver of the whole creation. These have become so infatuated with the idea of their self-sufficiency and superiority as *Brahm* or God that they adore no one as their creator or superior, and fearlessly act according to the dictates of their impure mind and senses; and as their bondage with the material covering or body and its various currents, continues unrelaxed, they are at the time of death hurled down into the regions of matter and find new bodies and places fit for their reception according to the result of their good and bad actions and their predominant passion or desire.

64. The proper course for a sincere lover of the Supreme Being is to acquire knowledge of the secrets and the order of creation and the

means of traversing the distance and stages between his dwelling in the body (the pupil of the eye) and the abode of the Supreme Being, the Prime Source of every thing; and to start on his journey with fervour and perseverance with the avowed object of one day reaching the presence of the Most High and Beloved Supreme Father.

Shabd or Word is not originally the result of vibratory motion or the property of ether as supposed by a certain class of thinkers.

65. There are some who regard Word or Sound as the quality of void or ether, while others consider it the result of vibratory motion; but they both labour under an erroneous impression. When it is asserted by all revealed religions that *Word* or *Sound* was the first manifestation of the Deity or Supreme Being, and the rest of the creation, including ether and other elements, was created by the *Sound* or *Spirit current*, how could then the original *Word* be regarded as the quality of ether, when it is the life and soul of every thing that followed its first manifestation. Again when the

original *Word* or *Spirit current* was the prime mover and the first impulse which came from the Supreme Source, and was the first cause of all sorts of motion and colours and forms, how could it be regarded as the result of vibratory motion which motion is, however, the subsequent expression or manifestation of spirit or energy throughout the creation. The vibratory motion is confined to the spheres where matter exists in subtle or pure or less pure and impure or coarse form and is the result of contact of spirit with matter; in other words, it is the manifestation of an effort on the part of the spirit current, descending from the highest sphere, to remove the material coating of the spirit or energy in the lower regions.

66. It should, therefore, be clearly understood that instead of sound being the result of vibratory motion, it is really the prime cause of everything in the Universe and also of vibratory motion, which again is instrumental in furthering the work of creation in the material regions. In the lower regions various sound

currents originate from vibratory motion and serve the purpose of carrying on the work of creation in various directions below; but the original sound or spirit current is the parent of all motions and forces as well as light, sound, elements &c., &c., that came subsequently into existence in the second and third grand divisions.

What is Truth ?

67. There are many who assert themselves to be searchers of Truth, but there are few who try and persevere to ascertain it, and fewer still who sincerely work at any sacrifice, to attain it. By Truth or *Satpad* is meant the Essence, Spirit, Soul, and Life of every thing that exists or appears to exist, itself unchangeable and immortal. Again, we might define Truth or *Satpad* as the Essence of Essences, Spirit of Spirits, Soul of Souls, Omniscient, Omnipotent, Formless, Boundless, Unapproachable, Unknowable (except by *Sants*), Unchangeable, Unfathomable, the Source and Beginning of life, of energy and of every thing (perishable and imperishable), an Unlimited Ocean of love and

wisdom, Omnipresent but concealed in various coatings except in one place viz., the highest region, where it can be observed by the spirit's visionary power.

68. The former definition is applicable to the Truth or rather to the rays which issued forth from the Sun of Truth or the drops from the unbounded Ocean of Truth diffused over all the space comprised within the Universe of Universes; giving life, power, and energy to bodies, existeers and appearances. By these rays is meant the spirits residing in all apparent bodies or existeers, forming the creation in various spheres in the space, and giving them the power of motion, thought or reason, &c., &c. In short, the whole creation extending from the highest to the lowest sphere, is sustained by the spirits or rays from the Sun of Truth, and disappears or is dissolved on the separation of spirits from the coatings or bodies in which they reside, or in other words, on the severance of the connection between the two.

69. The second definition points to the

source of the above rays or spirits, the Truth of Truths, ever shining forth in its awful majesty and splendour, and directing from its highest abode the course of its rays and controlling the forces which sprang up from their contact with matter and are playing their respective parts in the whole creation in the spheres below. To summarize the above, the whole creation which one feels, sees and observes, owes its origin, life and growth to Truth, and is sustained throughout by Truth, and disappears or is dissolved when Truth is separated or withdrawn therefrom.

How to attain or realize this Truth.

70. To approach the source of Truth one must first approach and catch its ray or spirit current and then follow and trace its course back to its source, the Truth of Truths. It is well said by some philosopher, "First know thyself (Spirit or Truth) and then know thy God (the Source of Spirits, the Truth of Truths)". The highway to reach the Truth and thence its source or the Truth of Truths, lies within the Microcosm or the human body.

71. It must be understood that the spirit current as well as the currents of other forces (spiritual-material) are flowing from within downward or outward towards external objects; and to approach their centres one must change the direction of these currents upward or backward to their internal source. As the stream of the spiritual material forces appertains to sensual desires or worldly pleasures and greatness, the traveller, bound for the regions of Truth, must, of necessity, give up these desires to a certain extent and thus shut up or stop its downward flow before he can safely proceed on his journey. It is not necessary that one should altogether withdraw from the world and its objects, but he should so regulate the course of the current of the various forces as to confine their use to what is absolutely necessary for living in this world with family &c., on a moderate scale, discarding all vain and improper or sinful ideas and acts.

72. Any one acting in the above manner will be able to gradually realize the Truth

within himself. But there are very few who would attempt to make the above sacrifice and regulate their habits and conduct to meet the conditions of the great enterprise they undertake; and hence the real Truth has remained concealed and unknown. Again, there are very few who would devote a portion of their time and attention to conduct enquiries earnestly to satisfy themselves of the existence of Truth and of the correctness of the means prescribed for its realization or attainment within their own selves.

What is true religion.

73. True religion or faith is that which leads a sincere enquirer to the regions of real Truth, and teaches him the ways and means of traversing the regions where false and untruth and comparative truth exercise their sway, and of finally reaching the highest and most sublime mansion where nothing but the Truth of Truths dwells and manifests its unrivalled glory in splendid refulgence and everlasting joy and happiness.

74. Any religion or faith which treats of rituals and ceremonies or external observances and moral principles &c., and does not profess to know, or can not teach the secrets of real Truth or the Truth of Truths, is a religion built on knowledge and reason or founded on scanty information furnished by revelation of a lower order emanating from the presiding spirit or genius of the second or third grand divisions where untruth and comparative truth hold sway.

What is true salvation.

75. The attainment of this Truth of Truths in its highest mansion, by a sincere and affectionate devotee, is called true and perfect salvation. There are many who, in their search for Truth, traversing some distance stopped short on their way in one or other lower sphere in the material regions, and regarded it as the mansion of Truth. Every one of these lower spheres is, however, the mansion of comparative truth and in the absence of instructions from a Perfect Guide or *Satgurú* many have been misled to regard

false or apparent or comparative truths as real and pure Truth; and the result is that they unwittingly remained in the material regions to die and be re-born after certain long periods.

76. Every higher sphere is the abode of the Master and Director of the creation of that sphere and of the spheres below, and is, therefore, more joyful and more lasting than the latter. But as far as matter extends there is no permanent durability and immunity from change, decay or dissolution; and, therefore, these spheres are unfit for the reception of a devotee who is desirous of approaching the Supreme Being, the Truth of Truths, the Joy of Joys, Unchangeable and Immortal, full of everlasting and unbounded bliss and felicity unalloyed with any form of matter.

Luminous and dark rays.

77. It may be observed here that rays of light (resplendent pure white light) represent Truth or Spirit in this world or, in other words, are originally emanations from the spiritual Sun of Truth; while darkness and dark rays represent

matter and instability or untruth, and are emanations from the luminous as well as the dark Suns. The rays of light are called luminous and those of darkness non-luminous. A sincere devotee should not stop at any stage where there are both light and darkness, but should continue his journey onward until he reaches the region of pure, eternal, resplendent light where there is no darkness at all, that is, the region of Truth and of pure Supreme Spirit.

78. In like manner and in correspondence with the above there are two currents flowing from the higher regions of the brain in the human body, viz., white matter and grey matter; the former being the representative of light and spirit, while the latter partakes more or less of matter and darkness. In the spheres comprised in the third grand division white light represents spirit current, while blue light and dark rays indicate *Kál Purush* or *Brahm*, the ruler of the coarse material regions.

79. The tendency of *Brahm* or the Universal Mind is downward and outward, and that

of matter or *Máyá* still more downward and outward as the latter forms the superficial covering of all bodies created in various spheres of the second and third grand divisions; hence the war of spirit with these two most powerful agents or factors in the creation which present grand obstacles and impediments to a devotee or pure spirit on his onward journey towards its source, the Supreme Being. These obstacles can easily be overcome only by the grace and mercy of the Supreme Father and the help of the *Sant Satgurú* or Mediator.

Absolute necessity for spiritual devotion.

80. It may be concluded from the above that so long as the spirit remains clothed in material coverings or bodies in the regions of matter (the second and third grand divisions), it will, of necessity, be subject to the forces of nature or matter which have a downward and outward tendency and that unless it withdraw its currents to a certain extent from the objective world, with the help of a Superior Spirit or *Sant Satgurú* (who has freed

Himself from the bondage of matter) and tries to traverse and raise itself above the material spheres by practising a certain mode of devotion, it cannot expect to liberate itself from the various material coverings and their influences and reach the pure spiritual regions, the abode of the Supreme Being, and thus attain perfect salvation.

81. It is, therefore, absolutely necessary for and incumbent upon every human soul, male or female, desirous of escaping the pleasures and pains of this world inseparable from the assumption of material body and also the excruciating pains of leaving the body and everything surrounding it, (the objects of its joy and pleasure) at the time of death, as also to avoid re-birth and the sufferings attendant thereupon, to search for a Superior Spirit or Perfect Guide, and under His guidance and benign influence start on its homeward journey with an ever increasing love for, and with a fervent desire to approach, the Supreme Father, and thereby secure His grace

and mercy for the easy and early attainment of its aim and object, the Holy Presence of the Supreme Being.

The work of salvation can be carried on in human body only—A devotee is not required to quit his family and profession.

82. The mode of devotion referred to can only be practised while a spirit dwells in a healthy human body and those who fail to accomplish the work of devotion or even commence it during their present life, must inevitably submit to a series of births and re-births in infernal regions of matter and to the suffering and pain inseparable therefrom. Any amount of regret, remorse or repentence at the time of death and after it, will be too late and of no avail. *And regret they must*, who fail in their present life to avail themselves of the opportunity offered them for regaining their lost kingdom, the abode of the Supreme Father.

83. If a man has not sufficient means of accomplishing the work of salvation in his present life he should not be discouraged

or disappointed. If he simply commences the work under the guidence and merciful protection of a *Sant Satgurú* and the Supreme Father, Rádhá Soámi, he will be able to accomplish it in the next, or one more subsequent birth which will be superior in every respect to the previous birth and when he will have sufficient means at his disposal to help him in finally attaining his object.

84. It must be clearly understood that Ráhdá Soámi faith does not require or permit any one who joins it, to quit his family or surroundings or give up his avocation or profession to obtain his livelihood; on the other hand it enjoins the advisability of a devotee continuing to live with his family and discharge his household and professional duties satisfactorily and at the same time secure salvation by earnestly and fervently practising devotion from two to four or at the most six hours a day, distributing the above time at the rate of half, three-fourths or one hour at a time according to his convenience.

The Sphere of true salvation.

85. A little consideration and careful observation of the affairs and the transitory state of this world will show that our abode on this earth is temporary and that our permanent dwelling is in the pure spritual regions and that so long as the spirit remains clothed in material body on this or any other globe in the material regions, it must suffer more or less mental or bodily pain and enjoy wordly pleasures to a greater or less extent, and be also subject to re-birth whether it takes place sooner or later, and that these vicissitudes of life in the lower spheres cannot be avoided until traversing the material spheres by devotional practice, the spirit returns to its happy home, the Holy Abode of the Supreme Being.

86. It becomes, therefore, absolutely necessary for all sensible human beings to exert themselves to quit the infernal material spheres and approach the Supreme Being in His highest and Holiest Mansion, without which perfect salvation cannot be attained.

Three powers of man—Physical, Intellectual and Mental, and Spiritual.

87. There are three powers latent in the human being, viz., (1) Spiritual, (2) Mental and Intellectual, and (3) Corporal or Physical. Every one of these powers requires regular training under a guide or master before it can be awakened, and brought into use for any purpose. The physical powers comprise the action of and the work done by the senses and limbs, such as the organs of sight, hearing, taste, speech, smell and touch &c., as also hands, feet, generative organ &c. Those who have developed any of the above senses or limbs to perfection and adopted them to special uses, such as drawing, painting, copying, singing, dancing, playing on musical instruments, riding, sleight of hand &c.,&c., can acquire name, fame, and earn good livelihood; whereas those who have remained dull and undergone no training of any kind, work merely as labourers, coolies or ploughman, and earn hardly sufficient to live from hand to mouth.

88. Again, those who have undergone

higher training and awakened their intellectual and mental power to perfection in any particular line or department of science, become literary men, philosophers, astronomers, statesmen, administrators, judges, barristers, doctors, engineers &c., and acquire greater renown and worldly power to control and direct the affairs and in fact rule the destiny of millions of people inhabiting various districts and countries. These functionaries are respected and obeyed by all and receive high remunerations for their intellectual work.

89. Again, those (though few in number) who have by continued practice of piety and devotion succeeded in awakening and developing their spiritual power have merited special grace and mercy of the Supreme Being and become prophets, mediators and saints appertaining to the second and third grand divisions and have done much for the salvation of human race. Their fame has spread far and wide and their name and person have in a manner become immortal and are adored and

regarded as the means of salvation by millions of people inhabiting distant lands and countries. They have, further, ascended heaven and enjoy the honour and happiness of remaining in the presence of their God; and while on earth they sometimes exercised extraordinary or supernatural powers.

90. It is left to the choice of human beings to undergo regular training under a competent master and use their best efforts to awaken and develop any of the above powers. There are many who do not care to make use of any of the above powers, while there are some who exert themselves earnestly to develop their intellectual or physical power. Nearly all seem to be indifferent to the necessity of awakening the spiritual power. But it is doubly, nay, absolutely, necessary for all human beings for the sake of their spiritual benefit, and to save their spirit from eternal perdition to exert themselves to the best of their powers to awaken and develop, at least to a certain degree, the spiritual power lying

dormant within their ownselves. If they do so, they will not only enjoy happiness and contentment and a healthy constitution in this world, but also secure heavenly bliss in the next, and escape various sorts of pains and troubles as well as the misery of re-birth, and eventually reach the presence of the Supreme Father in the Highest Heaven, and enjoy eternal happiness.

The advisability of awakening and developing spiritual powers.

OBSERVATION I.

91. The human spirit being native of pure spiritual regions and a denizen on this earth, it becomes necessary for its rest and comfort that it should try to return to its source where alone it can enjoy pure spiritual happiness permanently.

OBSERVATION II.

92. The human spirit being mostly attached and confined to this world through the senses of sight, hearing and taste, it can easily release itself from the bondage of body and pleasures

of this world by turning these very senses upwards within itself, whereby it could see higher objects, hear heavenly sounds, and taste the nectar of life which flows from higher regions in the brain.

OBSERVATION III.

93. There are many gentlemen and in some cases ladies too, who set out bravely at great risk of life and property on exploring expeditions to the Poles and various other unknown and untraversed lands and hills in distant parts of the globe, or ascend the sky in balloons or conduct experiments for the navigation of air, also for making new discoveries in chemistry, electricity and other branches of science &c., the fruits of which are a very small addition to the knowledge of geography or other department of science, and some personal advantage in the shape of fame and name to the adventurer. It, therefore, seems equally, nay, highly desirable, for the permanent and most important benefit of humanity in general, to start on a journey in

untrodden spheres, to ascertain the source, or in other words, the happy home of our own selves, viz., the spirit, and to reach the sublime presence of our beloved Supreme Father, the Almighty Creator. The adventurer will secure great and lasting reward, namely, the approbation of the Supreme Father, and salvation of mankind in general, and permanent immunity from re-birth and pains and pleasures of life on the earth.

OBSERVATION IV.

94. Every one burns with the desire to acquire worldly riches, sensual pleasures and worldly fame and greatness. There are many who toil and work hard to satisfy their ambition. Of these some succeed fully and some partially in their efforts, while others fail altogether. Those who are fortunate in attaining the object of their aspiration are again in constant anxiety to obtain more and more the object they have gained; and those who did not try their luck or make any attempt to acquire worldly wealth, pleasures and fame, burn with envy and jealousy

to see their more fortunate brethren in full or partial enjoyment of the same. Thus the whole lot of people always suffer from, or are tormented with, the pain of discontent, disappointment, jealousy and envy, or insatiable thirst or greed for more and more.

95. Again, all human beings are subject to four kinds of afflictions, viz., (1) mental, such as fear, anxiety, pain caused by mishap, theft, loss and bereavement &c., sorrow for a relation or friend in distress or trouble &c., &c., (2) various diseases of body and senses, (3) quarrel, enmity and dispute with others, (4) pangs of death.

96. Some of these cases are partly or wholly remediable, while others of serious nature are wholly irremediable and beyond the power and control of humanity. In these latter cases man can get no help from others and has to reluctantly suffer extraordinary pains, troubles and privations.

97. The most holy and sublime Rádhá Soámi faith prescribes remedy for both sorts of

troubles, namely, those mentioned in paragraph 95 as well as those in paragraph 96. The remedy is simple and can be applied by all if they will only willingly undertake (at no trouble to themselves) to practise devotion according to *Surat Shabd Yoga*, or in other words, try to liberate their spirit from the bondage of matter by raising it from its seat in the pupil of the eye towards its source, the highest sphere or pure Spiritual region, the abode of the Supreme Heavenly Father.

98. By doing so, all desires for worldly riches, pleasures, name, fame, power and greatness, will gradually cease and in lieu thereof will spring up intense love for the Supreme Being and a strong desire to approach His Holy Mansion and witness His glory in the creation.

99. In like manner the more the spirit disentangles itself from the bondage of body and other objects of this world, the less will it feel the effect of afflictions and adversity which generally befall mankind in this world,

and by the Grace of the Almighty Father acquire sufficient strength to withstand all temptations and privations in life and gladly meet death when it comes, in order to attain heavenly bliss in higher spheres and everlasting joy in the highest mansion of the Supreme Being.

100. There is no other way or means of overcoming or escaping the troubles and pains to which human life is subject in this world except the practice of concentration and sublimation or elevation of spirit to higher spheres according to *Surat Shabd Yoga* as prescribed by Rádhá Soámi faith.

OBSERVATION V.

101. The spirit current is constantly flowing out through the nine principal orifices or apertures in the body, viz., two eyes, two ears, two nostrils, mouth, generative organ, and anus, and is the cause of pleasures derived by senses &c. But these pleasant sensations are not lasting and the impressions produced by them on the mind are so numerous and

of such a conflicting nature that eventually they give rise to serious disturbances in the realms of thoughts and ideas.

102. A wise and prudent man should avoid lending his power of senses to promiscuous observation and collection of varied impressions and formation of indifferent and sometimes indistinct ideas therefrom, in view to keep down irregular, improper and unnecessary desires which spring up in the heart and prove a source of unlimited bother and trouble to the thinker.

103. Ordinary people out of curiosity take very little care to guard their senses against their misuse, but it is incumbent on all thoughtful men and women to exercise some restriction over their love of curiosity and to restrain the external flow of their spirit current through the senses by changing its course under the instructions and guidance of a *Sant Satgurú* or a *Sádh Gurú* towards the tenth higher orifice or aperture in the interior, through which the main spirit current flows

from its source in the higher regions of the brain into the body.

104. This change can be easily but gradually effected by following the practice of concentration and sublimation of mind and spirit according to the instructions given in Rádhá Soámi faith. It is nothing more than the following of the course or passage of the spirit which it adopts at the time of leaving the body (when death occurs), and if this work can be accomplished to a certain extent in life time it will be attended with very beneficial results in the end, in as much as it will not only save the practitioner from the excruciating pains &c., which are experienced by all at the time of death, but also enable him to witness the glory of the Supreme Father and through His Mercy and Grace secure abode in the happy and peaceful regions on High. All men and women of thought and wisdom should covet this reward and strive to obtain it through the medium of *Sant Satgurú* or one of His sincere and loving followers.

OBSERVATION VI.

105. People suffering from bodily and mental diseases run to doctors for remedy, and readily follow their instructions in taking medicine and food prescribed by them, and are very impatient to recover their health. But all persons more or less suffer from the effects of diseased mind and yet they are ignorant of the evil results that await them owing to the ever increasing unhealthy condition of the mind which entices and prompts them to commit (intentionally or unintentionally) sins and improper acts in word, in thought and in deed.

106. One can only become cognizant of this error and ignorance when he associates with divine and pious persons who constantly try to watch, control and check the evil tendencies of their mind and the improper desires springing up in their heart. And if he be inclined to get cured of this unhealthy and dangerous state of his mind he should have recourse to a *Sant Satgurú* or His sincere and

affectionate follower for remedy, for they are the doctors who are well acquainted with the diseases of the mind and can prescribe easy and effective means for their removal, by instructing the patient in the practice of concentration and sublimation of mind and spirit.

107. Taking into consideration the absolute necessity of the welfare of the spirit, it appears to be incumbent on all persons to take notice of the diseased state of their mind and to adopt necessary measures for remedying the evil within their present life-time, otherwise their case will become nearly hopeless and render them liable to great hardships and troubles in this life as well as in future re-births in the material regions to which their spirit and mind will remain confined.

Love for the Supreme Being.

108. This practice can be conducted easily and comfortably if the devotee has a little love for the Supreme Being. Without love it will be too hard and difficult to practise *Surat Shabd*

Yoga with any good result to be obtained within a short time.

(1) The Supreme Being, being a boundless Ocean of Spirit or Love and a human being, being a drop or current of spirit or love from this Ocean, and love being the very essence and means of existence of the whole creation, it follows that no effort in any direction, temporal or spiritual, unless actuated by *love* or affectionate regard, can be crowned with success, and the work or labour rendered easy, sweet and harmonious.

(2) Love is most sublime, having its origin in the highest region, the abode of the Supreme Being. In whatever heart it springs up, it will gradually raise and carry the fortunate possessor of this lofty and noble passion to the highest region.

(3) All good qualities and goodness itself will gradually find their home in the heart in which love dwells, and all bad qualities will be rooted out by and by.

(4) Whatever a man full of pure love

thinks or does is all wisdom, while the thoughts and works of worldly wise men are full of selfishness and folly.

(5) Knowledge without love for the Supreme Being is futile and tends towards untruth or darkness or materialism, while love turns every thing to good use and leads to enlightenment and truth. Even worldly love, such as filial and conjugal, is attended with goodness, happiness and comfort to all concerned. How much more good would then result to mankind in general if the same love become spiritual, and be directed towards the Supreme Being, the Merciful and Kind Parent of the whole creation.

(6) Self-love brings on egotism or pride, and sows the seed of hatred, jealousy and disregard in the minds of kindreds, associates and neighbours; while pure and sacred love for the Supreme Being creates in the heart humility, meekness and an affectionate regard for kindreds, neighbours and humanity in general.

(7) Pure and holy love is always ready to spend (regardlessly) whatever it has for the sake of its beloved, the Supreme Father, and the benefit of mankind without any distinction; whereas self-love or love of world always tries to appropriate every thing to itself, even at the risk and loss of others.

(8) Pure and holy love is always ready to sacrifice any thing whatever to gain admission into the presence of the beloved, the Supreme Being; whereas self-love will never part with any thing except for the sake of its own aggrandisement and indulgence in sensual pleasures.

(9) The noble passion of love is most powerful and strong. It removes all obstacles and thorns in its way and discards all superstitions, doubts and scepticism.

(10) Where pure love dwells there sheds the light of Grace, as it forms a link with the spirit or love current from its source, the Supreme Being.

(11) Such is the strength and effect of affection and kind treatment that it subdues ferocity and other injurious and dangerous characteristics in beasts and other animals, that is to say, they begin to love and have an affectionate regard for their keepers and trainers.

(12) A heart devoid of love or affection is as hard as stone, and does not form a suitable receptacle for the light of Heavenly Grace and Mercy.

(13) Sincere love is reciprocal, so if one has a heart full of love for the Supreme Being, he is sure to be attracted towards Him by Grace, Mercy and Holy Light which will gradually illumine his inner-self, and then all menial or worldly affections and desires will gradually disappear.

(14) Love or the power of attraction is the basis of the whole creation and the cause of its sustenance and preservation.

(15) The Supreme Being loves and takes special care of those who love Him with all

their heart and soul, and gradually draws them towards Himself, the grand centre of pure light and attraction; while those whose hearts are imbued with worldly love and passions recede from this centre, or in other words, they of themselves fly away towards the circumference or darkness and untruth.

(16) Every wave of love rising in a lover's heart brings tidings of goodness and joy from the beloved, and every thought springing up in such a heart is a harbinger of good works and good services for the sake of the beloved.

(17) Love has no bounds, knows no restrictions, and is not limited by conditions, and like its source is extensive and far-reaching in its beneficial results.

Faith.

109. Faith built on pure and sincere love for the Supreme Being is strong and immoveable like a mountain, and love founded on strong faith goes on increasing till it carries the lover to its fountain head, the Beloved Supreme Being. Both strong love and strong faith are

sure and certain means to the attainment of perfect salvation. They are inseparable from each other.

Incarnations.

110. It must be clearly understood that as the Supreme Being now and then incarnates Himself in the person of a *Sant Satgurú* or sends His special beloved sons as *Sants*, so does the viceroy or president of the second grand division or *Brahm* or Lord God appears in this world in the person of a *Jogeshwar* as first class incarnation, or sends his special sons or agents as *Sádhs* or first class prophets. In like manner, the governor or president of the third grand division incarnates himself in the person of a *Jogi* as second class incarnation or sends his agents as second class prophets. There is great confusion in the promiscuous use of these names, and very little or no distinction is made in the rank and powers of these superior spirits. In the Rádhá Soámi faith a clear line is drawn to distinguish the position and functions of each of these above

spirits, according to the height of the sphere to which they belong and from which they descend.

111. A follower of Rádhá Soámi faith who practises devotion according to instructions given by the *Sant Satgurú*, will pass through the spheres occupied by the superior spirits referred to above, on his journey to the highest sphere or the abode of the Supreme Being. He will, however, not loiter on the road or in the mansion of any of the above superior spirits, but with the help of Grace and Mercy of the Supreme Father and the *Sant Satgurù* proceed determinately, direct to his destination unimpeded by any obstacle thrown in his way by mind and matter, and unallured by any temptations offered by the varied creation in the intermediate spheres.

Necessity of a contemporary Sant Satgurú.

112. According to Rádhá Soámi faith the presence and help of a *Sant Satgurú* is absolutely necessary for a neophyte to commence the work of salvation, or in other

words, to practise internal devotion for the purpose of first concentrating and then raising his spirit beyond the material spheres.

113. All embodied spirits living here having left their original home from time immemorial, and having passed through various material spheres in their descent to the corporeal body in the third grand division, have become so firmly attached to their present dwelling viz., the body and its surroundings in this world, that it is difficult, nay, impossible, for any one to effect a change in the present condition and abode without the aid and instructions from One Who is a resident of that sphere and holds communion with the Supreme Father, because He alone can be expected to know all the secrets of the descent of the spirit to the lower regions and the means of liberating it from the bondage of matter to enable it to rise and return to its original source. Such a *Sant Satgurú* occasionally appears in this world for the salvation of fallen spirits.

114. There is no other means except by

associating with the *Sant Satgurú* and His affectionate followers to acquire love for the Supreme Being and practise devotion with an intense desire to approach Him and have a glance of His glory and resplendence in the highest sphere where He dwells.

115. Mere knowledge of the mode of devotion derived from hearsay or reading the holy books will not help a would-be traveller on his journey homeward; it needs full instructions from an experienced guide and occasional help and information from him to enable a novice to proceed on his journey unhampered by obstacles and impediments which are generally met with in traversing material spheres. When no worldly knowledge or art or profession of any sort can be acquired by any one without undergoing training under an experienced master, how could it then be possible for any one to acquire any knowledge of the Supreme Being and hold communion with Him without help and instruction from an experienced Master or Guide called the

Sant Satgurú, who would spiritually keep an eye on His disciple and watch the progress of his homeward journey to the spiritual regions and at the same time take care of him, so that he may not be tempted and detained by Superior Mind and matter or their agents on the road.

Distinguishing features of Sant Satgurú or True Guide.

116. As in these days there are many who call themselves *Sants*, *Sádhs* and guides or leaders of sects and religious societies &c., &c., it is difficult to distinguish between a *Sant Satgurú* or true Spiritual Guide and a host of family or ancestral guides and wandering mendicants and religious leaders, except by the means hereafter described.

(1) That the True Guide is He who imparts instructions for the practice of *Surat Shabd Yoga* as prescribed by Rádhá Soámi faith.

(2) That His object in preaching the holy doctrine and giving practical instructions is nothing more than the saving of humanity

from perdition and raising the human spirits to the highest and pure spiritual regions from which they originally descended.

(3) That He is not actuated to undertake this work from selfish motives or for any personal benefit or aggrandisement.

(4) That as envy and jealousy on the part of interested religious parties will try to slander His character and otherwise shower taunts and sneers on Him and His limited congregation, He wont feel ashamed or discouraged by such acts of the ignorant, jealous and worldly people, but go on with His sacred work steadily and determinately with full trust in the Grace and Mercy of His Beloved Father, the True Supreme Being who invariably extends His protection to the sincere lovers of Truth.

(5) That His discourses, being purely spiritual and full of affection for the Supreme Being, will be heartily attended to by sincere searchers of Truth and true lovers of the Supreme Being, and His instructions sought for by them to practise the mode of devotion

(*Surat Shabd Yoga*) calculated to raise the spirit to the Holy and Highest Mansion of the Supreme Father.

(6) That by acting up to His instructions, sincere lovers of Truth and the Supreme Being will derive much pleasure in their practice and have occasionally internal visions of supernatural character and glimpses of higher regions and also notice the Grace and Mercy and Protection of the Supreme Father now and then extended to them.

(7) That their belief and trust in the Mercy of the Supreme Father will go on increasing and strengthening, and with it also the love for the Supreme Father, imparting new strength and steadiness to the devotional practice.

(8) That as the practice and the joy thereby realized within increase, the mind of the sincere devotee will be gradually withdrawn from the world and its objects of pleasure, and regard all worldly hopes, joys and fears as worthless and transitory and feel unwilling

to devote more time and attention to them than what appears actually necessary for conducting business and family affairs.

(9) That by associating with such a Guide and hearing His discourses and attending to the practice enjoined by Him, all doubts and errors and improper impressions and reflections will be gradually removed from the mind of a sincere searcher of Truth, and his heart will accordingly be filled with pure love for the Supreme Being and His children, the humanity in general.

(10) That under His guidance a sincere devotee will be gradually able to control the action of his mind and senses as regards indulgence in worldly pleasures, and by and by forsake sins and sinful ideas; and should such thoughts ever enter his mind he will feel extremely sorry and from the bottom of his heart ask and pray for forgiveness and protection.

How a sincere devotee will act when he meets a Sant Satgurú.

117. A sincere and affectionate devotee

who has fortunately joined the congregation presided over by a *Sant Satgurú*, will readily offer anything, however valuable, for His service and will always be ready to gladly perform any service, however menial, that may be required of him on any occasion, and thus merit the Grace and Mercy of the Supreme Father and affectionate regard of the *Sant Satgurú.*

118. It is observed in this world that when one has strong friendship with or love for another, he is ready to sacrifice every thing for the sake of his friend or beloved; so in the religious world, when one fortunately meets a *Sant Satgurú* or a True Guide and under His guidance acquires strong love for the Supreme Being, he will act without reserve in doing what he possibly can to please the Supreme Father and the *Sant Satgurú*, which will show how much he values and what regard he has for purely religious duties in comparison to the worldly works and obligations.

Atheists labouring under a mistake.

119. Atheists who deny the existence of the Supreme Being or Creator and also of the spirit as emanation from the Supreme Being, appear to be labouring under a great mistake.

120. A reference to paragraphs 53–57 will show that there exists a Supreme Almighty Being, Who is the Original Cause and life and support of the whole creation and Whose unlimited power controls and directs the various forces forming the machinery thereof.

121. And again, the same paragraphs describe how the spirit, being an emanation from the Supreme Being by the power it inherits, summons all the forces of nature, elements, &c., on its first manifestation in the world to work harmoniously in constructing its receptacle, the body, and maintaining it in perfect working order as long as it occupies the same. In this case also the spirit force apparently controls and directs the action of the subordinate forces of nature &c., for the proper working of the machinery of the body,

and so soon as it is withdrawn, the whole machinery collapses and the form or body is dissolved and exists no more.

122. If the above facts do not fully satisfy an atheist he should at least take into considertion the change of states he undergoes daily (see paragraphs 44 and 45) whereby he will perceive that in his wakeful state he feels the pleasures and pains of this world; whereas in dream he is removed to another sphere which has little or no connection with the physical body and this world, and when removed further to the sphere of deep sleep he becomes in a manner unconscious, and the connection with the physical and astral bodies in a manner ceases. A little thought over these changes will enable him to notice that if he can by any means retire to the inner spheres at pleasure, he can find safety from all the pains and troubles of this world and the physical body, and at the same time enjoy greater pleasures and joys within himself without the least trouble and expense.

123. Every one, whether he be an atheist or otherwise, appears to be full of desire to obtain pleasures and greatness in this world, and to attain this object he works hard from his infancy to the time of death, whether his hope is wholly or partially realized or not.

124. Again, every one wishes to shun danger, sickness, ill-luck or any other mishap or misfortune and tries his best to avert it, or at least lessen its effect by any means in his power. Also every one fears death and the pain attendant thereon, and would try any means to avoid it as long as he could find it possible to do so.

125. A careful study of Rádhá Soámi faith will show that, if any person were to sincerely and affectionately practise devotion at least three hours a day, he would find that the mode prescribed by the Merciful Rádhá Soámi will gradually weed out all desires appertaining to this world by fulfilling some and showing the futility of others, and create a passionate love in his heart to approach the

Supreme Being and witness His Glory and enjoy real happiness in the heaven above and also give him strength enough to overcome the troubles and afflictions in this life and also the pain of death.

126. Thus the sublime and holy Rádhá Soámi faith and its practice fully meet the requirements of human beings, and should therefore be unhesitatingly adopted by all who, without renouncing this world, hope to secure perfect salvation or happiness in the next.

Matter and Motion.

127. Scientists say that Matter and Motion are the principal factors in the creation. This is true so far as the lower material regions are concerned, but they do not or cannot say how or whence this motion originated. Motion needs a motor, and this motor is the same spirit or word current issuing forth, like rays from the Sun, from various centres or spiritual-material Suns and diffused over all the space comprised in the second and third grand divisions.

128. Every atom is in itself a ray or current issued from a centre and is endowed with spirit power which (in this world) is called energy by the scientists. Unmanifested energy or spirit power is called *latent* or *potential*, and that brought into action or full play, *kinetic*. Both the above names apply to the impulse from the spirit force which is the origin and beginning of all.

129. The atoms playing their part in this world, for instance, issue forth from our Sun or the Sun above, of which the former is a planet. They are manufactured in the above orbs before they issue forth as rays or currents and are thus fitted for the work of creation or for forming parts of the bodies they combine to form or give existence to. The spirit current latent in these atoms is much steeped in matter of the lower spheres and it requires impulse from a higher current appertaining to and descending from the higher sphere to awaken its energy or actuate it into action.

130. It will thus be seen that spirit power

or force is all in all, or it is the principal factor or actor in the whole creation, or in other words, it is the life and soul of every thing.

Transmigration of soul.

131. Rádhá Soámi faith recognizes transmigration of soul or spirit, for so long as the spirit remains confined to the second and third grand divisions it must remain clothed in some sort of body or covering; and when one body is worn out it must of necessity assume another in the higher or lower spheres or sub-divisions according to its acts and predominant passion or desire.

132. We notice in this world that people of a peculiar turn of mind or taste invariably associate with, and find pleasure in the company of people of the same sort. So in the world to come, every one will be drawn or attracted to the sphere and company of those with whom he has sympathy or affinity owing to the common object of their desire and affection, and assume similar or different bodies according to the degree of their affinity and the result of their past actions or *Karma.*

133. Until, therefore, a spirit tries, by practising devotion according to the mode prescribed by Rádhá Soámi faith, to liberate itself from the bondage of matter and body predominant in the second and third grand divisions, and after closing its account of *Karma* rises to the highest sphere of pure spiritual region (called the first grand division), it cannot get rid of the material covering or body, and therefore it must continue subject to birth and re-birth, or in other words, the spirit must successively change its covering or body.

Description of Karma—reduction and obliteration of their effects.

134. There are three kinds of action or *Karma*, viz., first *Kriyamán* or the acts performed by a person in his present life, second *Prálabdh* or the acts performed in the past or present life, the fruit of which is to be reaped in the present life, third *Sanchit* or the unripe acts done in the past and present lives, the result of which is to be experienced in future lives.

135. A follower of Rádhá Soámi faith by

practising devotion and observing the rules prescribed by it can easily, though gradually, overcome or reduce the effect of all these *Karmas* and then get rid of the body, or break through the shackles of matter in the material spheres.

136. The rules to be observed are as follows :—

(1) That a sincere devotee *should resign himself wholly to the Mauj or Will and pleasure of his Beloved Father, the Supreme Being*, and thus leave the effect of all action or *Karma* done by him in the present life (according to the moral principles laid down in paragraphs 38 and 39) to be produced by *Mauj* so as to suit his spiritual and temporal interests, or in other words, give up his own personal desires and hopes and make them subservient to the Will of the Supreme Being. He will thus be freed from the effects of one sort of *Karma* called *Kriyamán.*

(2) As regards the second sort or *Prálabdh Karma*, their effects must of course be

experienced during the present life, but there would be a vast difference in the result (or the amount of pain and pleasure to be experienced) according to the progress made by the devotee in the spiritual practice and the degree of his love for and trust in the Mercy of the Supreme Father; because a devotee who is capable of withdrawing his spirit current inward and upward to a certain extent, will be less liable to bodily pains and worldly anxieties, fears and hopes, than a worldly or unpractised man whose spirit cannot move from its seat in the pupil of the eye except under the influence of sleep.

(3) *Sanchit Karmas* can be easily disposed of by a devotee during his practice. There are two sorts of impressions made on the mind's atmosphere, viz., (1) those produced by external objects when they come into contact with the senses, and (2) those produced by desires and various thoughts and ideas springing up from time to time in the mind. These impressions are strong or feeble according to

the intensity or weakness of desire and thought, or the force or indifference with which the senses grasp the external objects.

137. When a devotee is traversing the mental sphere on his journey homeward, these impressions are vivified by the power of spirit and appear to him as real objects; they engage or attract his attention and detain him for sometime, but as the devotee is forewarned not to busy himself with these impressions, he sooner or later breaks his connection with them and proceeds onwards whereby the spirit current is withdrawn from the above sphere and the said impressions rendered lifeless and incapable of producing any effect on the devotee when he returns to his seat in the body, viz., the pupil of the eye, after completing his devotional practice for the day.

138. It will thus be observed that the effect of *Sanchit Karma* is nearly obliterated after engaging the actor or devotee's attention for a few minutes only, instead of occupying days and months and perhaps years in some cases,

during the actor or devotee's next life, had he not been initiated in the *practice* prescribed by Rádhá Soámi faith.

Description of four Principal Personages concerned in the practice of Rádhá Soámi faith.

139. The Rádhá Soámi faith recognizes three Grand Personages, and a sincere and affectionate disciple the fourth, namely, (1) the Supreme Father, (2) the Supreme Mother or Original Spirit or Word current emanating from the Supreme Father, (3) the Supreme Son or *Sant Satgurú*, the Representative of the Supreme Father in human form, (4) the disciple or the son or human spirit.

140. The above quaternity may be further explained as follows:—

The first personage or the Supreme Father and Sole Master is a vast and Boundless Ocean of Spirit and Love and Joy from Whom the Original Spirit or Word current emanated. The second personage or the Supreme Mother is the Original Spirit and Sound current, the prime mover, creator, nourisher and supporter of the whole creation. It is the connecting link between the Supreme Father and the son or disciple, and leads the way and helps the son in returning to the Father's Highest Mansion. The third, the Supreme Son or *Sant Satgurú* is the Representative of the Supreme Father in human form on this earth. This incarnation of the Supreme Father or His Special and Beloved Son *Sant Satgurú* appears now and then in this world for the purpose of saving spirits from going down to the lower regions and raising them to the higher spheres, and finally to the Mansion of the Supreme Father. The fourth, the disciple, the son or human being is a ray or drop descended from the Supreme Sun or Boundless Ocean of Spirit, Love and Joy; but his attention having been diverted by mind and matter towards the material creation down below, he has lost all knowledge of the Supreme Father and His Highest Mansion, and cannot now return to His Holy Abode without the help, externally, of Supreme Father or His Special and Beloved Son assuming human form of a *Sant Satgurú*, and internally, of the Supreme Mother or the connecting spirit and sound current between the Supreme Father and the disciple or son Who illumines the heart of a sincere lover and devotee and sheds grace and mercy upon him.

141. As the disciple or devotee proceeds on his journey homeward, he gradually absorbs the spirit and sound current, or in other words, shortens the distance between himself and the Supreme Father, and thus playing in the lap of the Supreme Mother, he returns with his loving Mother to the Holy and August Presence of the Supreme Father.

142. Without the help and Grace of the Supreme Father, and His Special and Beloved Son, the *Sant Satgurú* in human form, no human being can ever acquire sufficient strength to give up worldly desires and pleasures or to undertake the journey homeward, or in other words, practise devotion according to the mode prescribed by Rádhá Soámi faith. It must always be remembered that none but the *Sant Satgurú* can under His own protection,

regenerate fallen humanity and grant sufficient strength to enable a disciple or devotee to fight his way out of the various spheres presided over by Superior Mind and matter, where all sorts of obstacles and temptations are ready to interrupt the traveller in his journey and draw him towards the creation in higher spheres on the way.

The work of regeneration.

143. The work of regeneration consists in the movement of spirit and mind from the lower to the higher spheres by the practice of devotion. A man may be said to be twice or thrice born according as he has traversed the regions appertaining to first, second or third birth. A sincere devotee having strong love for the Supreme Being, may, through perseverance and fervour and with the Grace and Mercy of the Supreme Father and the *Sant Satgurú* of his time, traverse the regions of two or three births in one life-time, that is to say, raise his spirit to the second grand division, and complete the work of regeneration

in the next life by undergoing the fourth birth or traversing the spheres appertaining thereto, and finally enter and take his abode in the Mansion of the Supreme Father at the top of the first grand division or pure spiritual regions.

Rádhá Soámi faith is open to all mankind who may or may not renounce their old creed.

144. All people without any distinction of caste, creed and colour can be admitted into Rádhá Soámi faith; and as the devotional practice appertaining thereto is conducted mentally and spiritually, it is not binding upon the followers of this faith to publicly renounce their former creed and its external observances, or in other words, it is optional with them to do so or not according as they can easily overcome all opposition and obstacles in their way, or find it difficult and inconvenient to face them in the beginning; internally, they must, however, adhere to the practice prescribed by Rádhá Soámi faith, which they can easily attend to, unnoticed by others, at the time they have to be present with their family and friends

at the performance of the rituals or ceremonies of their old creed.

People desirous of seeing miracles &c. unfit to follow Rádhá Soámi Faith and practise devotion prescribed by it.

145. People are generally very fond of seeing miracles or acquiring supernatural powers, and with this object in view they express their readiness to practise any mode of devotion and even to sacrifice (temporarily) all sensual pleasures and desires for greatness in this world &c., &c.; But this is a mistake, and they are labouring under a delusion; and as such persons cannot be regarded as sincere searchers of Truth or lovers of the Supreme Being, the Rádhá Soámi faith does not accept their overtures for admission and initiation into its secrets.

146. A sincere devotee having no other object in his view than to approach the Supreme Being in His Highest Mansion, will, however, witness glories of the Supreme Father in various forms on his way to his destination, and see many things more

wonderful than ordinary miracles, if he will only practise devotion for sometime with strong faith, fervour and love for the Supreme Being. He will further observe the Grace, Mercy and Protection of the Supreme Father extended to him on all occasions when needed.

147. A member of Rádhá Soámi faith is strictly forbidden to divulge the secrets or mention to any one (even to a fellow member without express permission) the glory and wonder of the higher creation he sees now and then within himself, or the happiness and extraordinary joy he experiences during his practice, or the special Mercy, Grace and Protection extended to him from time to time on important occasions by the Supreme Father and *Sant Satgurú.*

Published by

Facsimile Publisher
Ashok Vihar, Delhi-110052 (India)
Website: www.facsimilepublishers.com

Distributed by

Gyan Books Pvt. Ltd.
5, Ansari Road, Daryaganj, New Delhi-110002 (India)
E-mail: books@gyanbooks.com, Website: www.gyanbooks.com

9 789333 664547